I0766206
THIS BOOK BELONGS TO:

MEZZO
ZENTANGLE
DESIGNS

MEZZO
ZENTANGLE
DESIGNS

MEZZO
ZENTANGLE
DESIGNS

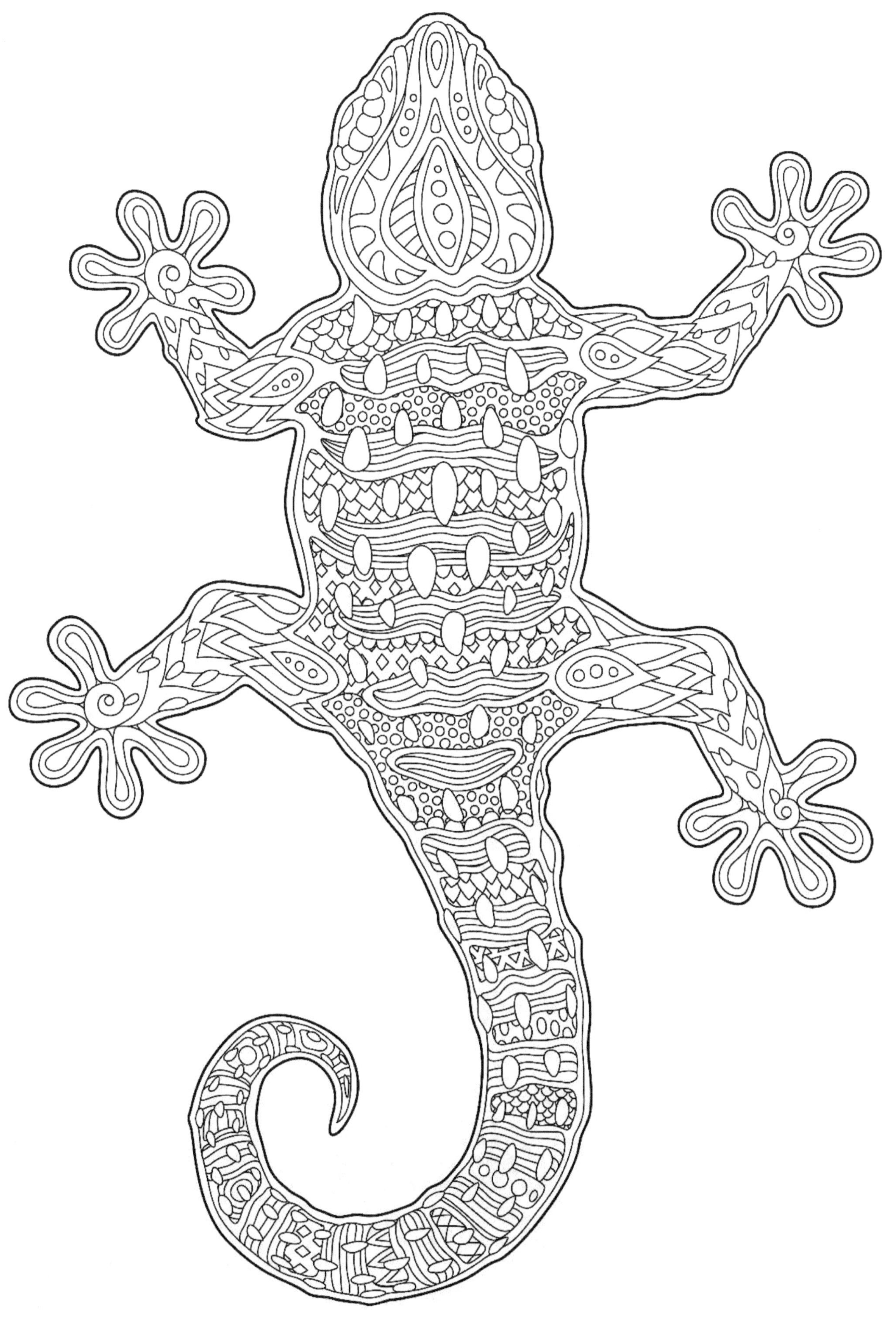

MEZZO
ZENTANGLE
DESIGNS

MEZZO
ZENTANGLE
DESIGNS

MEZZO
ZENTANGLE
DESIGNS

MEZZO
ZENTANGLE
DESIGNS

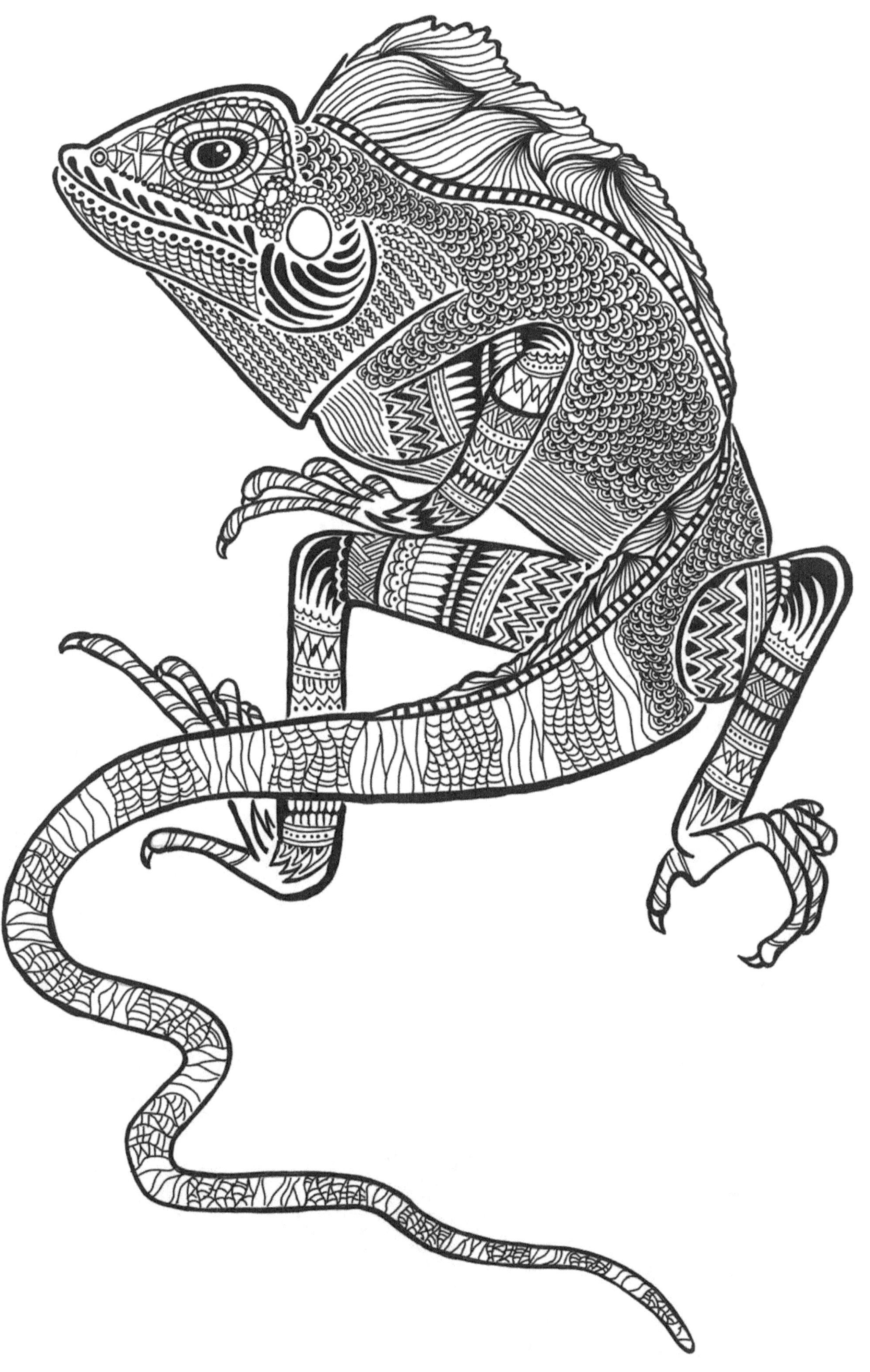

MEZZO
ZENTANGLE
DESIGNS

MEZZO
ZENTANGLE
DESIGNS

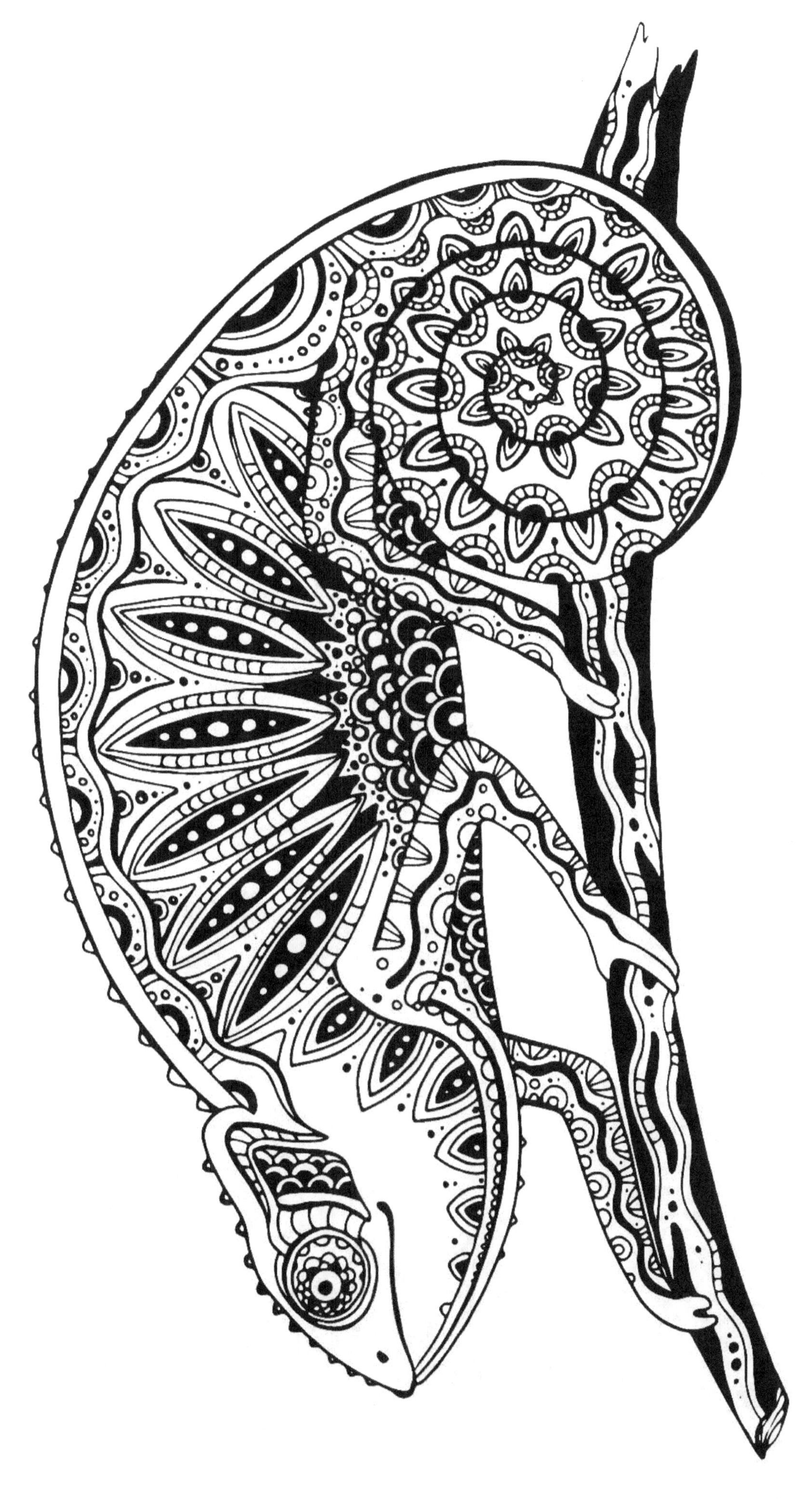

MEZZO
ZENTANGLE
DESIGNS

MEZZO
ZENTANGLE
DESIGNS

MEZZO
ZENTANGLE
DESIGNS

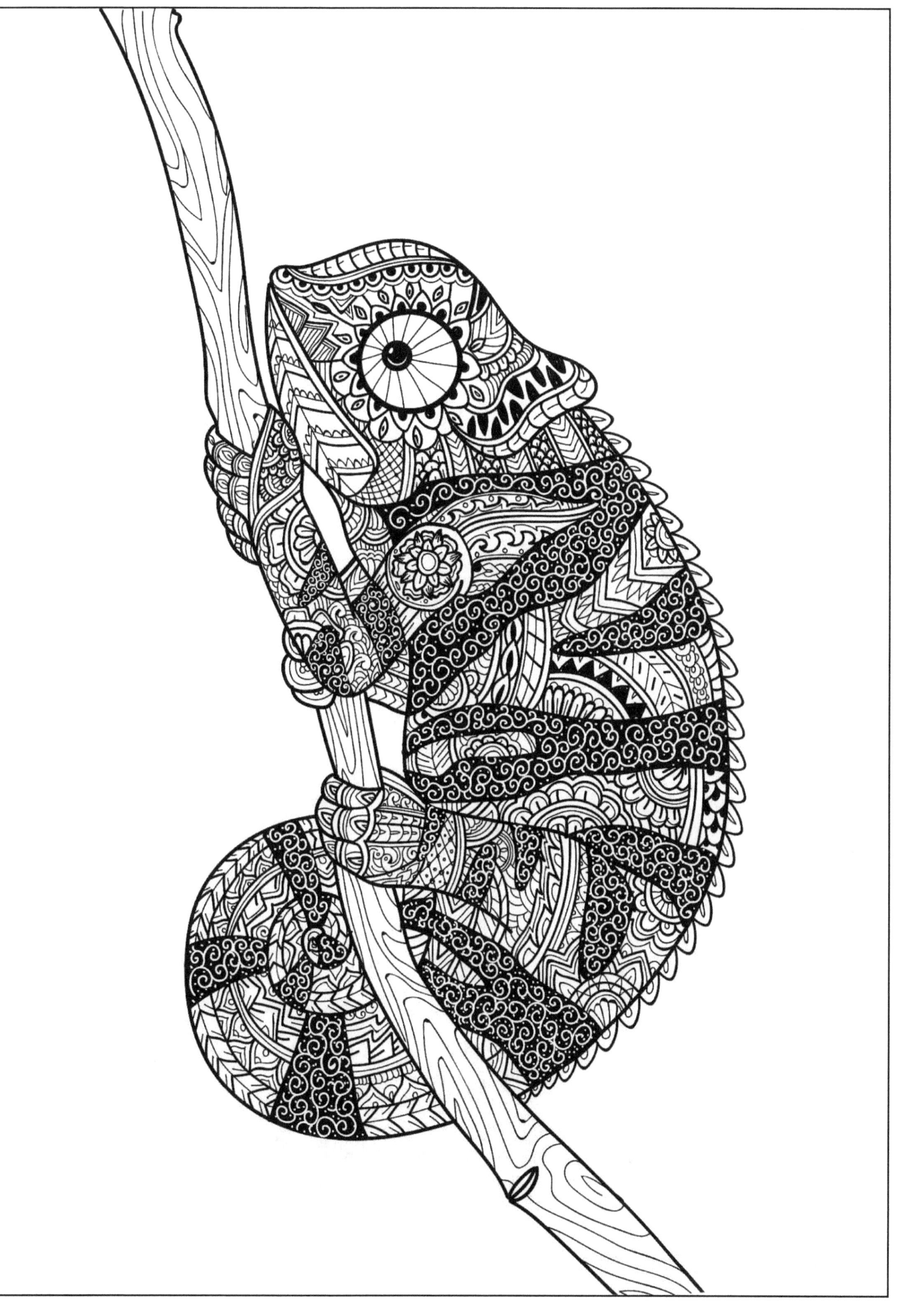

MEZZO
ZENTANGLE
DESIGNS

MEZZO
ZENTANGLE
DESIGNS

MEZZO
ZENTANGLE
DESIGNS

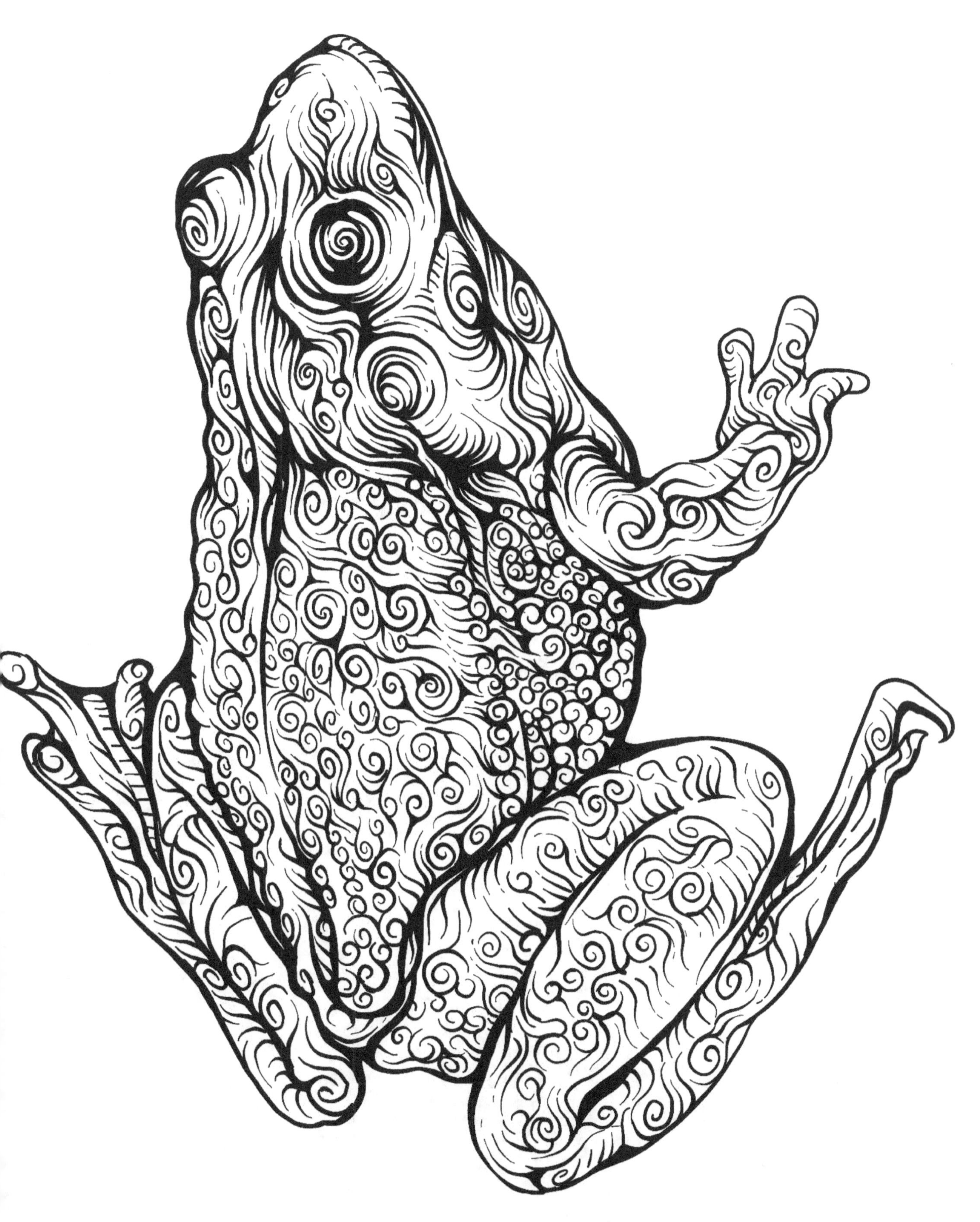

MEZZO
ZENTANGLE
DESIGNS

MEZZO
ZENTANGLE
DESIGNS

MEZZO
ZENTANGLE
DESIGNS

MEZZO
ZENTANGLE
DESIGNS

MEZZO
ZENTANGLE
DESIGNS

MEZZO
ZENTANGLE
DESIGNS

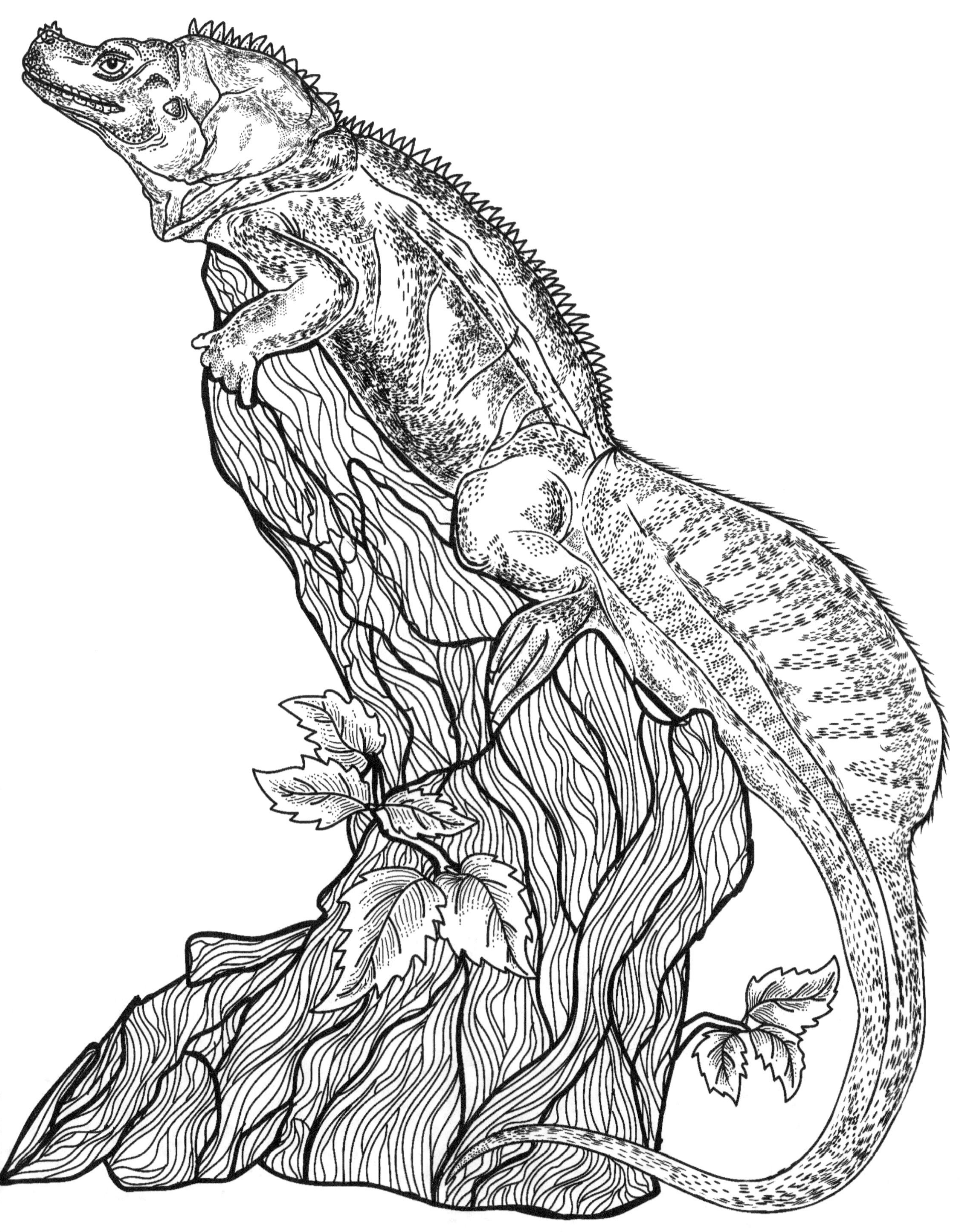

MEZZO
ZENTANGLE
DESIGNS

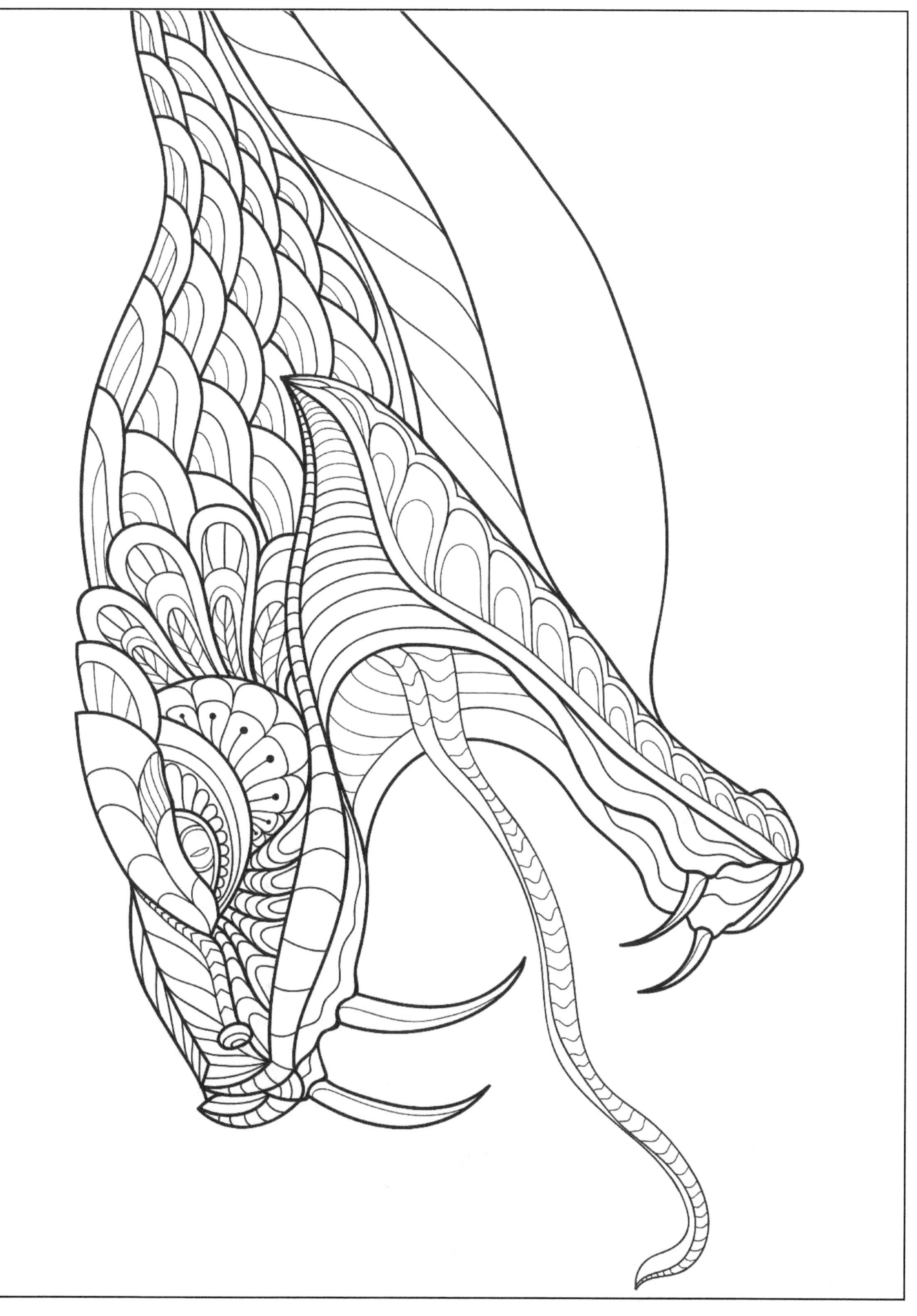

MEZZO
ZENTANGLE
DESIGNS

MEZZO
ZENTANGLE
DESIGNS

MEZZO
ZENTANGLE
DESIGNS

MEZZO
ZENTANGLE
DESIGNS

MEZZO
ZENTANGLE
DESIGNS

MEZZO
ZENTANGLE
DESIGNS

MEZZO
ZENTANGLE
DESIGNS

MEZZO
ZENTANGLE
DESIGNS

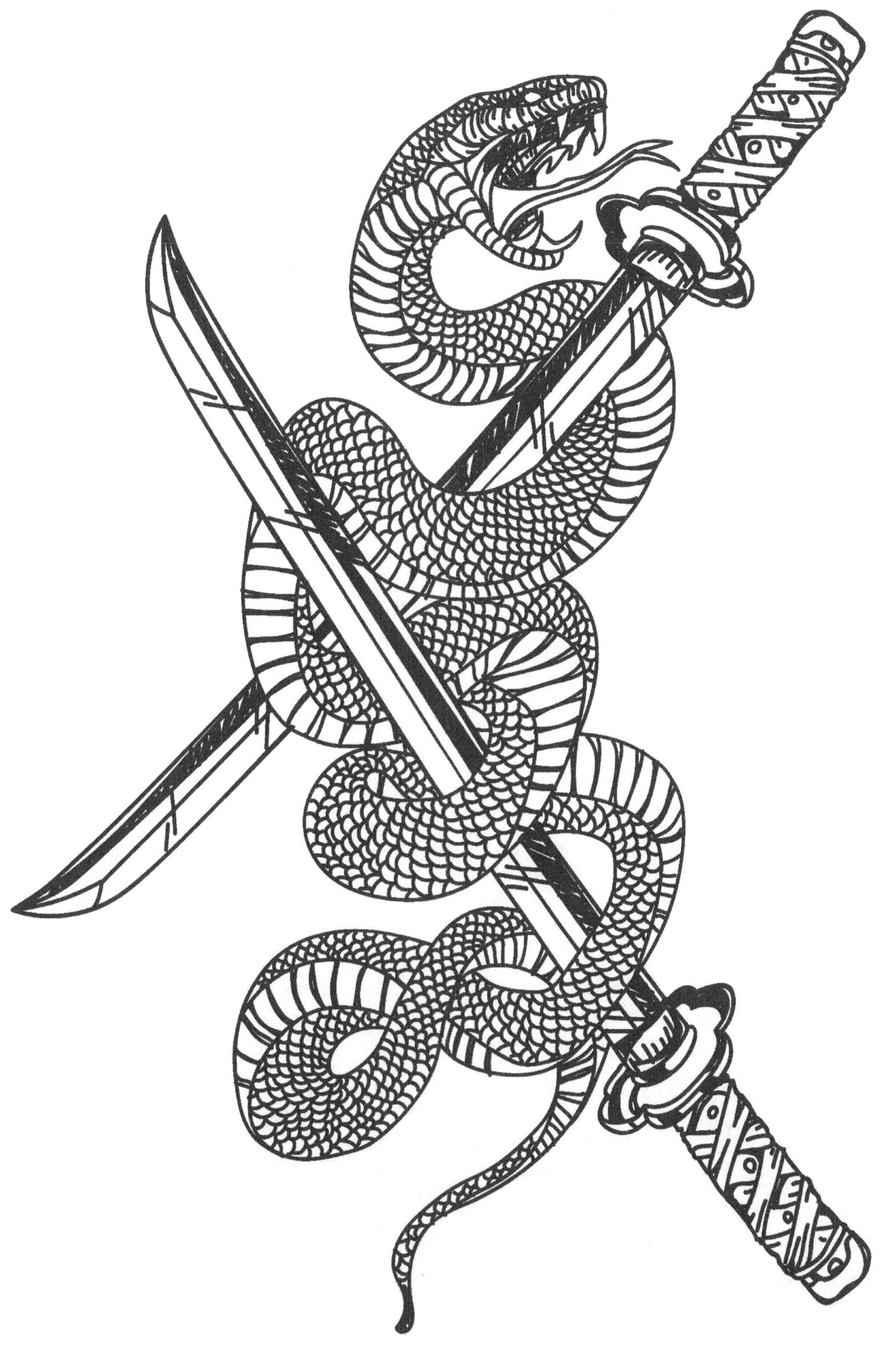

MEZZO
ZENTANGLE
DESIGNS

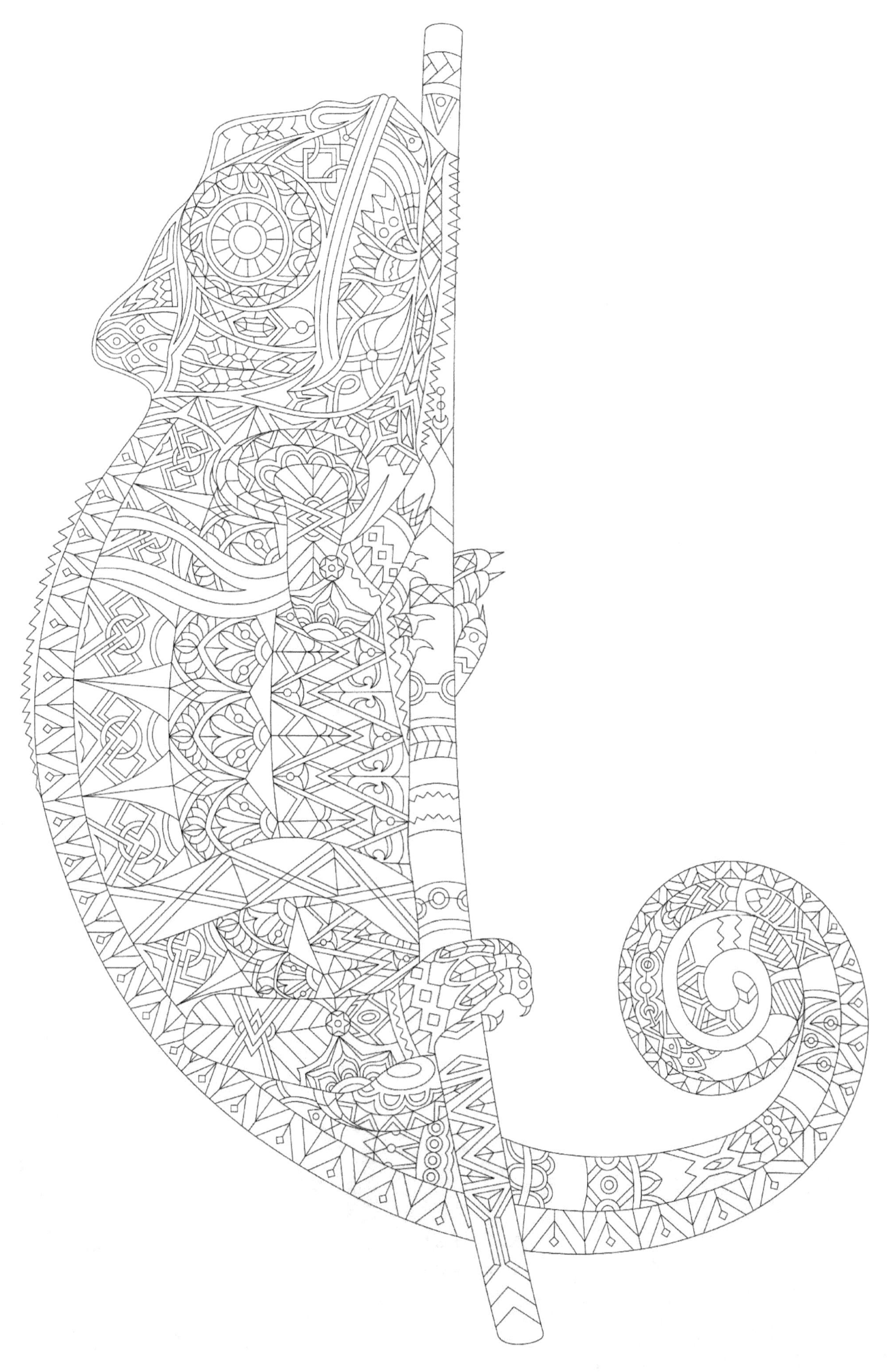

MEZZO
ZENTANGLE
DESIGNS

MEZZO
ZENTANGLE
DESIGNS

MEZZO
ZENTANGLE
DESIGNS

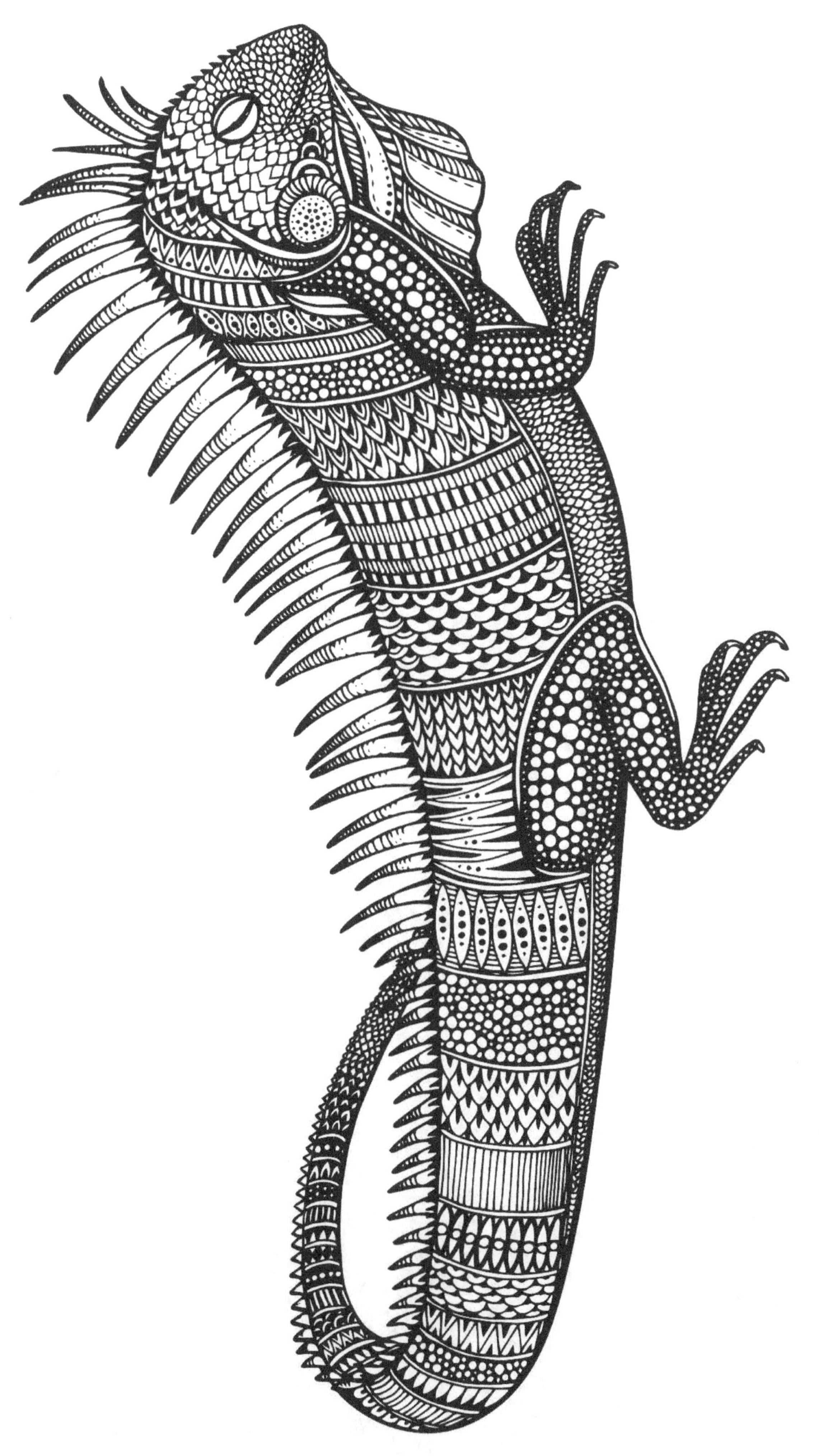

MEZZO
ZENTANGLE
DESIGNS

MEZZO
ZENTANGLE
DESIGNS

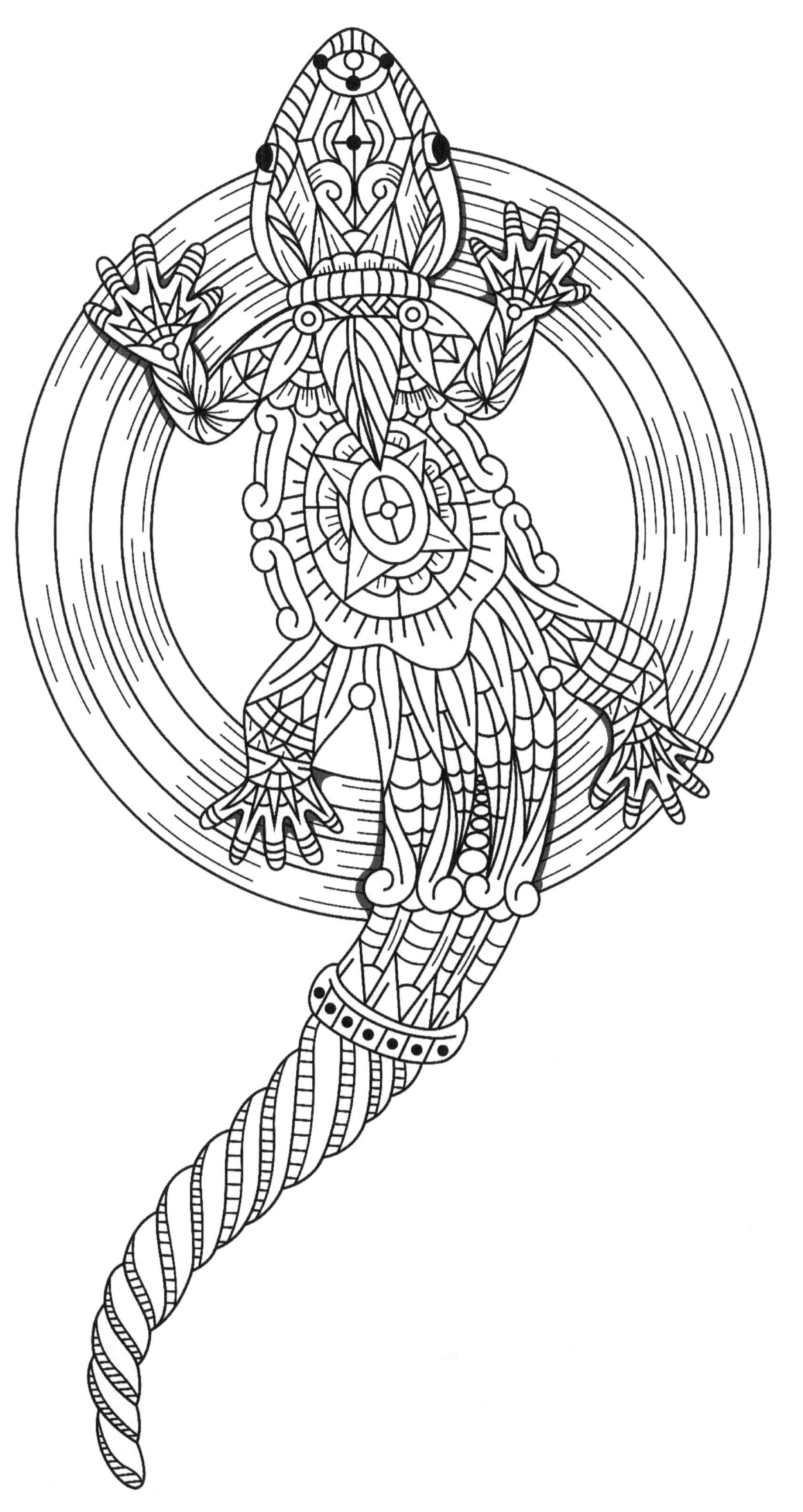

MEZZO
ZENTANGLE
DESIGNS

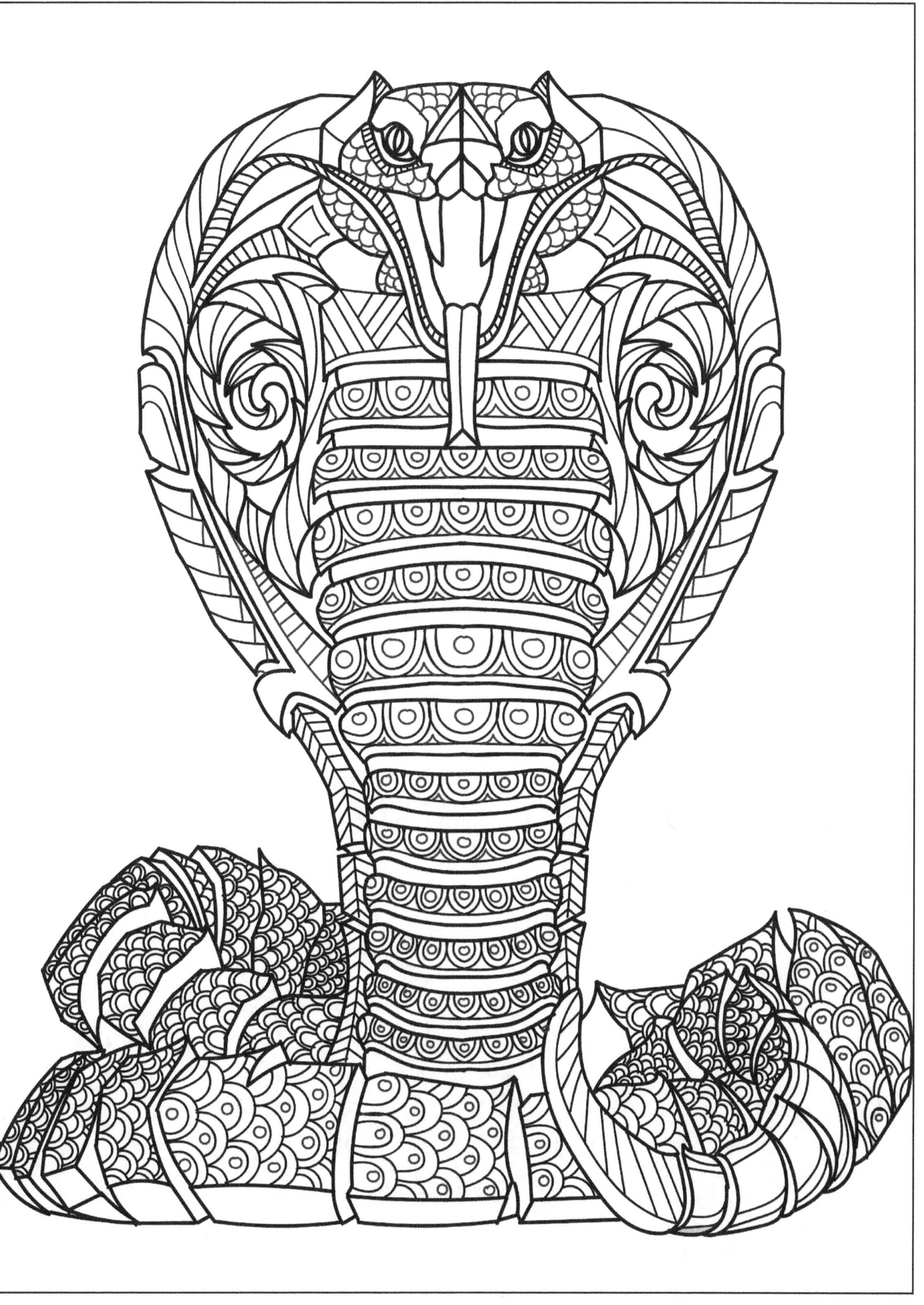

MEZZO
ZENTANGLE
DESIGNS

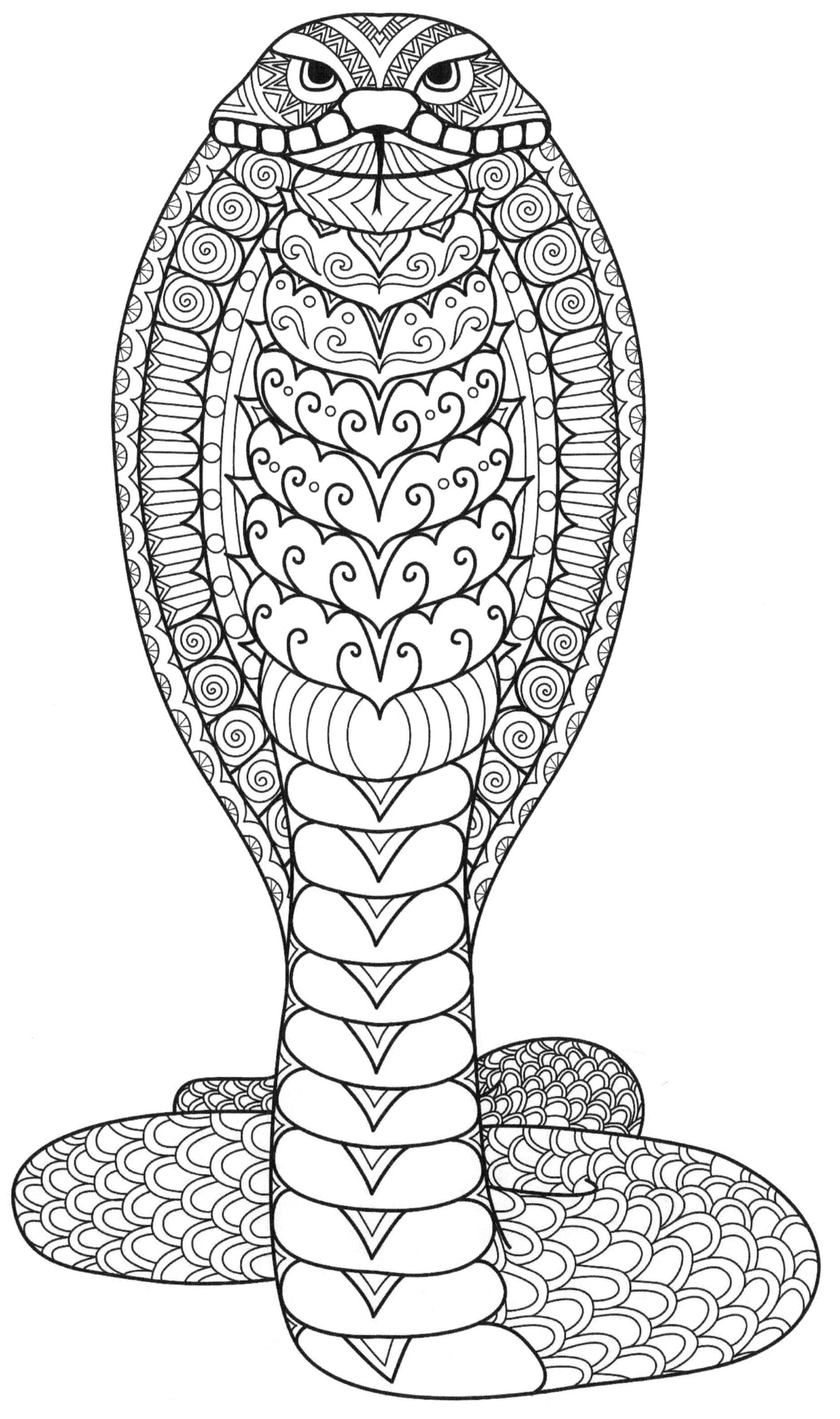

MEZZO
ZENTANGLE
DESIGNS

MEZZO
ZENTANGLE
DESIGNS